Delicious Vegan Macrobiotic Desserts

ERIC LECHASSEUR

love, eric

ISBN 0-9772937-0-X

Book design by Ellison/Goodreau
Edited by Holly Prado and X-tine Goodreau
Creative consulting by Sanae Suzuki

All photographs by Yoshi Ueda,
except page 8 photograph by Hideaki Wakimoto,
and page 45 by Eric Lechasseur

The ceramic dishes used in the following
photographs were handmade by:
Sanae Suzuki, pages 12, 64
Vladimira Zboril, pages 14, 36, 46, 72, 84
Michiko Nakamura, pages 20, 68, 74
Eric Lechasseur, page 78

For my teacher,

my best friend,

my soul mate,

and my wife, Sanae

CONTENTS

ACKNOWLEDGEMENTS

Having seen this recipe book through to completion, I find myself wanting to thank many people. Some have made major contributions to this book directly; others have been helpful to me in different ways.

For making this book possible, I would first like to thank my wife Sanae Suzuki for all the hard work, for her vision, which is the essence of the book and for continually pushing and critiquing me; my parents for always believing in and supporting me; Madonna, for her continued support of both of us; Michio Kushi and the fondly remembered Aveline Kushi for providing the foundation this book is built on; my first macrobiotic counselor, the late Cecile Levin; Juliet Hohnen for suggesting that I focus entirely on pastries for this volume; Mayumi Nishimura for being such a dear friend; Ruska Porter for believing in me; Nadine Burner for exposing me to beautiful macrobiotic desserts in the beginning of my macrobiotic cooking; Karen Person and Laura Garett for continuing to ask, "When will the pastry cookbook be ready?"; Vladimira Zboril and Michiko Nakamura for the lovely ceramic plates; Mike Nakamura for his support; Jeff Liu, Doug Clayton, and long-time good friend Judy Lee for correcting my English!; all my non-macrobiotic friends and neighbors (especially Marty and Nancy Hamaluk) for being the guinea pigs for my creations; my photographer Yoshi Ueda for his good eyes; Christine Goodreau and Mike Ellison for the graphic design work and for all the help they've been over the years; and especially to "the Golden Girls," my dogs Kin, Dore and Kula, for being so willing to help me "clean up" after all my cooking disasters.

Without these friends and family I would not have been able to make this book — it is a product of all of our efforts together. Thank you.

FOREWORD

I love desserts. If it's sweet, I'll try it. As a founder of the natural foods movement in the United States and after more than fifty years of dedication to a macrobiotic lifestyle, I am thrilled that more and more ways are being found to marry healthy, natural foods with delicious dessert recipes like those you will find in this book. Trying these recipes will be an amazing, rich journey for you – your biggest challenge will be to keep from going overboard and making them all at once!

When macrobiotic foods were first introduced to the United States in the 1960's, they were presented as recovery foods that could help ailing people regain their health. The formulas for setting a macrobiotic diet were somewhat rigid and strict; thoughts of taste and variety were afterthoughts rather than important elements of the lifestyle. This presentation of macrobiotics was appropriate at the time, but as that generation of macrobiotic practitioners has grown older and a new, younger generation has arrived, it is time for macrobiotics to change, to adapt to the new times. Macrobiotic foods now must become appealing visually, tastefully and aromatically as well as providing a way for people to live naturally, happily, and peacefully.

In this cookbook, Eric Lechasseur clearly understands this new way of thinking of natural foods and how to excite people (including me) about how delicious and appealing macrobiotic foods can be. This book contains Eric's "love letters" to his wife, Sanae – a collection of beautiful, tasteful macrobiotic pastry recipes. As you read the following pages, then try some of the recipes yourself, you cannot help but sense the love, joy and excitement that Eric has put into each one. Nothing can boost your own love life more than presenting a freshly-made *Apple Tart Tatin* to your spouse or significant other on a romantic evening!

I met Eric Lechasseur in September of 1997 at a macrobiotic fund-raising dinner for the Smithsonian Institute. He and his wife, Sanae, were volunteering as chefs for the event. He had only been exploring macrobiotic cuisine for a short time, mostly to help his wife recover from a bout of cancer she had had a few years before. Did he have any idea that eight years later he would be one of the leaders in the macrobiotic crusade? Maybe only his wife knew at the time. Already an expert in Japanese and French fare, he has now worked with experts around the globe to fuse those cuisines with macrobiotic philosophies, to develop his own unique cooking style. Eric and Sanae's dedication to healing through macrobiotic foods and the macrobiotic life style has nurtured their individual spirits, their personal relationship (they married in June of 2004, after more than thirteen years of friendship), and their interactions with friends and family everywhere.

Welcome to Eric's world of macrobiotic desserts. I hope this cookbook will deepen your appreciation of the way natural foods can expand and enrich your life for years to come.

Michio Kushi
*The world leader of Macrobiotic education
for health and peace,
Brookline, Massachusetts*

A NOTE FROM ERIC

My first cooking experience was making sugar cookies when I was six years old with my grandmother in one of the coldest winters that I can remember. I lived east of Quebec in the town of St-Luce — a town no one has ever heard of who isn't from there. My parents both worked, so I started cooking at an early age for my younger brother and myself. Somehow, as a young boy cooking didn't bother me — especially when I got to choose what delicious food to make! I loved cooking sugar pie and any other desserts as often as I could.

I became a French chef at the age of nineteen. My focus shifted to other types of food, leaving my love of desserts behind in my childhood. I didn't think about making desserts or pastries again until I met my wife, Sanae, in 1991. She loved sweets, and she would often ask me to make some desserts. She clearly didn't understand the difference between a chef and a patissier, but instead of arguing with her I would make things here and there to keep her satisfied. I was never really interested in making pastries until she was diagnosed with ovarian cancer in 1993.

Sanae started to study macrobiotic cooking to heal herself from the cancer, but she was often sick and craved sweet desserts. However, vegan and macrobiotic desserts were uninspiring, much less appetizing. She would ask me to bring desserts from the restaurant where I used to work in Venice, California. Of course, they were not macrobiotic, so after she ate the desserts her condition would get worse, but when she started feeling better she wanted to eat sweet desserts again. She repeated this pattern over and over. It was frightening. It frustrated me to see her getting sicker and sicker while struggling to heal herself. She went to see a macrobiotic counselor, Cecile Levin, then had to stop eating any sweets and stick to macrobiotic healing food. I was already helping her to cook macrobiotic food on a daily basis, so one day I decided to try some macrobiotic desserts for her. It was a simple *Simmered Apple* with a pinch of sea salt. Since she had not eaten any sweets for a while, she was very happy and showed me her beautiful smile. I think it was that smile that made me really want to make more macrobiotic desserts for her.

Sanae's determination and strength, combined with my cooking, helped her slowly get better. Before long she was healthy and had finished a one year intermediate cooking course at the East West Macrobiotic Center with Cecile Levine. In the meantime, I was facing my own health problem. For a long time, I had had a serious skin condition, but since it only surfaced once in a while I did not pay attention to it. When it did flare up, I would just go to see the doctor and get cortisone shots. In the beginning of 1994, my skin problem came back. This time, it was very bad. My hands were so itchy that I even thought about changing my career, since I could not use my hands to cook anymore. I was getting the shot every other day and felt incredibly weak. Sanae was telling me to try a macrobiotic diet, but I was not able to give up my orange juice or espresso in the morning in favor of miso soup. Although I like miso soup, at the time I did not enjoy eating it first thing in the morning! These days, I eat it every morning. Believe it or not, I feel great! I think it was in May of that year I went to see Cecile Levin for myself and decided to try macrobiotics for a short time. It was not easy to make the transition in a fast-food world, yet the basics of macrobiotics were sensible and simple to follow for me. After three months, I was cured! I have had no problems since then, as long as I eat macrobiotic food and live macrobiotically.

In April of 1995, Sanae recovered from her cancer. She was hired at Erewhon Natural Foods Market in Los Angeles as a Macrobiotic Food Consultant. She started to teach cooking classes there, helping many people heal themselves. I, of course, became one of her best students.

The universe has many plans for us. Sanae and I feel that we are very fortunate to have been given the chance to study macrobiotics and to experience a new life together.

Enjoy making macrobiotic sweets!

Eric Lechasseur
Santa Monica, CA

ENJOY THIS SPRING TEA

Ryokucha (Green Tea):
Due to its antioxidant properties and its ability to
lower cholesterol levels, Ryokucha is one of the
most popular teas of 21st century. Green tea has
significantly less caffeine than either black tea or
coffee, while still retaining its energizing qualities.
It has a beautiful green color and a refreshing
aroma reminiscent of spring.

Makes 1 cup
1 heaping teaspoon Ryokucha (Green Tea) Leaves
1 cup purified water

Bring the purified water to a boil. Pour the
purified water over the tea leaves in a teapot and
let steep for 2 – 3 minutes. Strain and drink hot.

spring

Carrot Cupcakes with Caramelized Lotus Root

Meyer Lemon Pie

Pain Perdu with Lavender Roasted Kumquat and Soy Vanilla Cream

Spring Lady Peach Cobbler with Coconut Sorbet

Strawberry Mousse Cake

carrot Cupcakes with Caramelized Lotus Root

Spring baby carrot and lotus root are a unique and eye-catching combination.

MAKES 12 CUPCAKES

For the Caramelized Lotus Root:
48 thin slices of lotus root, cut into half
    moons
1 pinch sea salt
3 tablespoons maple syrup

For the Carrot Cupcakes:
1 ¾ cups unbleached flour
1 ¼ cups pastry flour
1 tablespoon aluminum-free baking
    powder
1 teaspoon baking soda
1 pinch sea salt
1 cup maple syrup
⅓ cup safflower oil
1 cup soy milk
½ teaspoon organic apple cider
1 teaspoon vanilla extract
½ cup walnuts, chopped
2 cups carrots, shredded
¼ teaspoon ground cinnamon
¼ teaspoon allspice
¼ teaspoon powdered cloves
¼ teaspoon nutmeg, freshly ground

For the Raisin-Lotus Stew:
¾ cup organic raisins
1 cup water
1 teaspoon kuzu

To make the Caramelized Lotus Root:
1. Boil the lotus root slices in water with a pinch of sea salt for 20 minutes. Drain and dry with a towel.
2. In a saucepan over medium heat, combine the lotus root slices with maple syrup. Cook until the maple syrup has almost evaporated. Transfer to a tray and allow to cool.

To make the Carrot Cupcakes:
1. Preheat the oven to 350°F. Lightly oil a muffin pan.
2. In a large bowl, sift together the dry ingredients.
3. In a blender or using a hand mixer in a medium bowl, blend the wet ingredients.
4. Add shredded carrots and stir to combine.
5. Pour liquid mixture into the flour mix. Using a wire whisk, gently mix wet and dry together. Do not overmix.
6. Pour the batter equally into each compartment of the muffin pan and place a few slices of Caramelized Lotus Root on top of each one. (This should use up about half of the lotus root slices).
7. Bake for 25 to 30 minutes. The cupcakes are ready when a bamboo skewer inserted in the center comes out clean.
8. Remove from the oven and allow cupcakes to sit in the pan for 10 minutes. Remove cupcakes from pan and set them on a wire rack to cool.
9. Serve cupcakes with the Raisin-Lotus Stew on the side.

To make the Raisin-Lotus Stew:
1. Dissolve the kuzu in 1 tablespoon of water and set aside.
2. Combine the raisins and water in a saucepan and cook gently over a low flame for 15 minutes.
3. Stir in the kuzu and remove the saucepan from heat. Add the remaining Caramelized Lotus Root and set aside.

meyer lemon pie

This pie uses the sweet, soft-skinned Meyer lemon, which is Sanae's favorite lemon. It is always light and refreshing, using amazake as a sweetener in this version.

MAKES 1 PIE

For the pie crust:
1 cup spelt flour
¾ cup unbleached flour
¼ teaspoon sea salt
⅓ cup maple sugar
⅓ cup safflower oil
¼ cup water

For the lemon filling:
1 cup plain amazake
1 ½ cups lemon juice
¼ cup rice syrup
¼ cup maple syrup
1 teaspoon vanilla extract
zest of 1 lemon
2 ½ tablespoons agar flakes
4 tablespoons arrowroot
¼ cup organic apple juice
extra lemon zest for garnish

To make the pie crust:
1. Preheat the oven to 350°F.
2. Combine the dry ingredients in a large bowl.
3. Add the oil and water, and knead quickly to form a dough. Allow dough to sit for 15 minutes.
4. Using a rolling pin, roll the dough into a circle to fit a 9-inch pie pan. (Dough thickness should not exceed ¼-inch).
5. Gently line the pie pan with the dough and bake for 20 to 25 minutes. Remove from the oven and allow to cool.

To make the lemon filling:
1. Combine all the ingredients, except for the arrowroot and apple juice, in a saucepan. Bring to a simmer and cook for 8 minutes, whisking constantly.
2. In a small bowl, combine the arrowroot and the apple juice, then whisk into the lemon filling.
3. Continue cooking and whisking a few more minutes. Remove from flame and allow to cool slightly.
4. Pour the filling into the baked pie shell. Garnish with lemon zest around the edges and refrigerate until firm.

 pain perdu with Lavender Roasted Kumquat and Soy Vanilla Cream

French toast was my favorite breakfast as a child. I thought you might love it as a dessert with lavender flavored Meiwa Kumquat.

MAKES 2 TO 4 SERVINGS

For the Lavender Roasted Kumquat:
12 kumquats
2 tablespoons rice syrup
1 teaspoon organic lavender flowers*
2 tablespoons water

For the Soy Vanilla Cream:
2 cups soy milk
½ cup rice syrup
¼ vanilla bean, split in half lengthwise
1 tablespoon kuzu
1 pinch sea salt

For the Pain Perdu:
4 slices of 2-inch thick sourdough bread
6 ounces firm tofu
1 cup soy milk
¼ cup safflower oil
¼ cup rice syrup
½ teaspoon ground cinnamon
1 pinch sea salt

Do not use lavender from a florist. Choose home-grown or organically grown flowers.

To make the Lavender Roasted Kumquat:
1. Preheat the oven to 350°F.
2. Add the 2 tablespoons of water to a small oven-proof skillet. Combine the kumquats, rice syrup and lavender flowers in the skillet.
3. Bake for about 15 minutes, basting occasionally with the liquid.
4. Remove from pan and set aside.

To make the Soy Vanilla Cream:
1. Combine vanilla bean and soy milk in a sauté pan and simmer for 5 minutes.
2. With a slotted spoon, remove the vanilla bean. Scrape the seeds from the bean and pour the seeds back into the soy milk, along with the rice syrup and sea salt.
3. Dissolve the kuzu with 1 tablespoon of water and whisk into the soy milk mixture. Cook over a low flame for 1 minute (do not boil).
4. Transfer the mixture to a container and refrigerate.

To make the Pain Perdu:
1. Combine the tofu, maple syrup and soy milk in a blender and process until smooth.
2. Add the remaining ingredients and blend for a few more minutes.
3. Transfer mixture to a large bowl.
4. Soak the slices of sourdough bread in the mixture for a few minutes.
5. Bring a sauté pan to medium heat and oil the bottom.
6. Remove any excess mixture from the bread slices and cook until golden brown, about 1 minute on both sides.

To serve:
1. Place each slice of Pain Perdu on a plate and top with the Lavender Roasted Kumquat and its cooking juices.
2. Pour the Soy Vanilla Cream over the kumquat as desired and sprinkle with lavender flowers.

spring lady peach cobbler

with Coconut Sorbet

Use fresh and ripe organic peaches to bring out their natural sweetness. Also delicious with rice ice cream.

MAKES 4 TO 6 SERVINGS

For the peach filling:
8 organic peaches
1 cup organic apple juice
3 tablespoons kuzu
1 teaspoon vanilla extract

For the cobbler topping:
2 cups organic rolled oats
¼ cup organic oat flour
½ cup maple sugar
⅓ cup safflower oil

For the Coconut Sorbet:
1 can organic coconut milk
½ cup organic apple juice
4 tablespoons rice syrup
1 pinch sea salt
1 vanilla bean, split in half lengthwise

To make the peach filling:
1. Preheat the oven to 375°F.
2. Cut the peaches in half and remove the pits. Slice each peach into eight sections.
3. Combine the peaches and apple juice in a saucepan. Bring to a boil and simmer for 5 minutes.
4. In a small bowl, dissolve the kuzu in 2 tablespoons of water.
5. Add the vanilla and kuzu to the simmering peaches, and cook for a few more minutes.
6. Remove from heat. Pour into a 9 by 12-inch baking pan and set aside.

To make the cobbler topping:
1. Combine the topping ingredients in a bowl and sprinkle over the peach filling in the baking pan.
2. Bake until topping turns a golden color, about 20 minutes.

To make the Coconut Sorbet:
1. Combine the vanilla bean and the apple juice in a saucepan, and simmer for 5 minutes.
2. With a slotted spoon, remove the vanilla beans. Scrape the seeds from the beans and pour the seeds back into the apple juice.
3. Add all the other ingredients to the apple juice, whisk well and transfer to an ice cream maker. Follow the manufacture's instructions for making the ice cream. (Chilling times may vary, usually 20 to 30 minutes.)
4. Add a scoop of the sorbet ontop of each individual serving of warm cobbler.

strawberry mousse cake

What a nice, refreshing cake, a staple in French desserts.

MAKES 1 CAKE

For the vanilla genoise:
2 cups pastry flour
2 cups unbleached flour
½ teaspoon sea salt
2 teaspoons aluminum-free baking
     powder
¾ cup safflower oil
1 cup soy milk
1 ¼ cups maple syrup
1 cup organic apple juice
1 tablespoon vanilla extract

For the strawberry mousse:
3 cups (20 ounces) fresh or frozen
     organic strawberries
12 ounces soft silken tofu
1 tablespoon tahini
½ cup rice syrup
3 ½ tablespoons agar flakes
½ cup organic apple juice

For the strawberry glaze:
4 ounces organic sugar-free
     strawberry jam
3 tablespoons water

To make the vanilla genoise:
1. Preheat the oven to 325°F.
2. Combine the dry ingredients in a large bowl.
3. In a separate bowl, combine the wet ingredients.
4. Using a spatula, pour the wet mixture into the dry and combine.
5. Line a 12 by 17-inch baking pan with waxed paper and spread the cake batter about ½-inch thick.
6. Bake for 20 to 25 minutes.
7. Remove from oven and allow to cool.
8. Flip the cake upside-down, remove the pan and peel the waxed paper off.
9. Slice 2 pieces of cake lengthwise that are 2-inches wide. Set aside.
10. Using the bottom of an 9-inch springform pan as a guide, cut the remaining cake into a circle.
11. Put the springform pan back together. Wrap the 2 strips of cake along the inside vertical edge of the pan to form the upper "sides" of the cake.
12. Press the circular cake piece into the pan to form the "bottom" of the cake. The "sides" and the "bottom" of the cake should meet snugly to provide a bowl-shape to hold in the mousse. Set aside.

To make the strawberry mousse:
1. Purée the strawberries in a blender.
2. Add the tofu, tahini and rice syrup. Blend until super smooth. Set aside.
3. In a small saucepan, bring the apple juice and agar to a simmer. Continue cooking until the agar is dissolved.
4. Pour the apple agar mixture into the blender and blend for a few more minutes.
5. Pour mixture into the cake mold. Refrigerate until firm, about 2 hours.

To make the strawberry glaze:
1. Dilute the jam with the water to make a thin consistency.
2. Using a stainless steel spatula, cover the mousse with a thin layer of the jam mixture. Refrigerate until ready to serve.

ENJOY THIS SUMMER TEA

Mugicha (Barley Tea):
This tea is served chilled during the summer, but
should not be over-iced. In fact, it can be enjoyed
at room temperature or hot to complement the
pastry and desserts. It has no caffeine. This tea
can be purchased in a Japanese market.

Makes 1 cup
2 teaspoons Mugicha
1 cup purified water

Simmer 2 teaspoons dry-roasted, unhulled barley
in 1 cup purified water over a medium-high flame
until dark brown (about 5 minutes). Stir
constantly. Strain before serving. If you wish to
roast your own barley, spread the barley on a
cookie sheet and bake in an oven at 225 degrees
for several hours.

summer

Almond Sablé Napoleon with Raspberries

Blueberry Pine Nut Pie

Grape Kanten Terrine with Pomegranate Syrup

Chocolate Raspberry Charlotte

Strawberry Sorbet with Crispy Almonds Tuiles

Upside-Down Berry Cake

Watermelon Thyme Granite

almond sablé napoleon with Raspberries

I love fruits and cream, so this is my version of the Napoleon pastry.

MAKES 4 SERVINGS

For the almond sablé:
1 cup pastry flour
1 cup organic oat flour
¼ teaspoon baking soda
1 pinch sea salt
1 cup almonds, finely ground
¼ cup safflower oil
¼ cup maple syrup
1 teaspoon vanilla extract
½ teaspoon almond extract
Sliced almonds for garnish

For the almond parfait:
24 ounces extra firm silken tofu
 (Mori-Nu brand)
8 ounces organic almond butter
½ cup maple sugar
¼ cup soy milk
1 tablespoon vanilla extract
Juice from 1 lemon
2 cups fresh organic raspberries
1 bunch apple mint

To make the almond sablé:
1. Preheat the oven to 375°F.
2. In a large bowl, combine the dry ingredients.
3. In a large cup, whisk together the wet ingredients.
4. Add the wet mixture to the bowl and mix well to make the dough.
5. Divide the dough into 2 pieces.
6. Place a sheet of waxed paper on a flat surface. Place ½ of the dough onto the paper and cover with another sheet of waxed paper.
7. Using a rolling pin, roll dough to ¼-inch thickness. Remove the top sheet of wax paper.
8. Using a knife, score the dough into 2 by 4-inch pieces, making sure not to cut through the paper. Remove the excess dough trimmings.
9. Sprinkle with sliced almonds. Carefully slide the waxed paper and sablé onto a 12 by 17-inch baking sheet.
10. Bake for 12 to 15 minutes.

To make the almond parfait:
1. Carefully drain and dry the tofu.
2. In a food processor, combine the tofu, almond butter, maple sugar, soy milk, vanilla extract and lemon juice and process for 2 to 3 minutes.
3. Transfer to a bowl and refrigerate for 1 hour.

To assemble and serve:
1. Place one 2 by 4-inch piece of the almond sablé on a plate. Arrange raspberries around the edge of the sablé.
2. Place 2 to 3 tablespoons of the parfait in the center. Repeat, creating another layer. Top with another sablé and dollop of parfait. Garnish with apple mint.

blueberry pine nut pie

This wheat free pie shell is versatile and can be used with any fresh berries of your choice. You will love it.

MAKES 6 SERVINGS

For the pine nut filling:
1 ½ cups pine nuts
2 ounces silken tofu (Mori-Nu brand)
4 tablespoons organic apple sauce
1 teaspoon aluminum-free baking powder
⅛ teaspoon sea salt
¼ cup rice syrup
1 teaspoon vanilla extract
2 tablespoons grapeseed oil

For the pie crust:
1 ¾ cups spelt flour
¼ teaspoon sea salt
⅓ cup maple sugar
⅓ cup safflower oil
¼ cup water

For the blueberry topping:
1 ½ cups fresh organic blueberries
1 cup organic apple juice
1 tablespoon kuzu
1 tablespoon agar flakes

To prepare the pine nuts:
1. Preheat the oven to 200°F.
2. Roast the pine nuts lightly on a baking sheet in the oven just until lightly golden in color, approximately 4 to 5 minutes. (Or toast pine nuts on the stovetop in a skillet.)
3. Transfer roasted nuts to a food processor and grind into a fine powder.

To make the pie crust:
1. Increase oven temperature to 350°F.
2. In a large bowl, combine the dry ingredients.
3. In a small bowl, emulsify the wet ingredients then combine with the dry mixture.
4. Knead quickly and allow dough to sit for 10 minutes.
5. Roll out the dough to fit six 4-inch pie shells or one 8-inch pie shell. Bake pie crust for 10 minutes and set aside.

To make the pine nut filling and pie:
1. Add the remaining ingredients to the pine nuts in a food processor and process until smooth.
2. Pour the mixture into the pie shell. Bake for 20 minutes.

To make the blueberry topping:
1. In a saucepan, combine the apple juice with the agar over medium-high heat. Simmer until agar has dissolved, about 5 minutes.
2. In a small bowl, dissolve the kuzu with 1 tablespoon of water.
3. Whisk the kuzu mixture into the apple juice and continue cooking and whisking until mixture thickens.
4. When it has fully thickened, turn off the heat.
5. Add the fresh blueberries to the saucepan and stir the mixture with a spatula.
6. Pour over the baked pie.
7. Allow the pie to cool before serving.

grape kanten terrine with Pomegranate Syrup

Great summer refreshment to soothe your palate. Try it with any other seasonal fruit.

MAKES 8 SERVINGS

For the grape kanten:
4 cups organic grape juice
½ tablespoon agar powder
1 pound organic red grapes, peeled

For the Pomegranate Syrup:
1 cup pomegranate juice
¼ cup organic apple juice
1 pinch sea salt

Seeds of 1 pomegranate, for garnish

To make the grape kanten:
1. In a saucepan, combine the grape juice and agar. Simmer on medium heat for 8 minutes and set aside.
2. Slice half a pound of the peeled grapes. (Each grape should be cut into approximately 4 pieces.)
3. Place the sliced grapes into individual 4-ounce ramekins or molds and pour the grape juice mixture over them to fill each mold.
4. Refrigerate for 2 hours.

To make the Pomegranate Syrup:
1. In a sauté pan, combine the remaining whole peeled grapes, pomegranate juice, sea salt, and apple juice over medium heat.
2. Continue cooking until liquid has reduced, about 20 minutes (or until the consistency of syrup). Set aside.

To serve:
1. Spread 2 tablespoons of the Pomegranate Syrup on a plate.
2. Unmold the kanten and set in the center of the plate.
3. Sprinkle with pomegranate seeds as garnish and serve.

COOKING TIP:
For people who like a more pliable texture for their kanten, use less agar powder but also use a shorter, flatter mold. When using other fruits, strawberries are the most versatile.

chocolate raspberry charlotte

Here is a popular combination, chocolate and raspberry. This is a favorite of many of our friends.

MAKES 1 CAKE

For the chocolate Lady Fingers:
¾ cup pastry flour
¾ cup unbleached flour
½ cup cocoa powder
½ teaspoon sea salt
¾ teaspoon baking soda
¼ cup safflower oil
⅓ cup soy milk
¾ cup maple syrup
½ teaspoon apple cider
½ tablespoon vanilla extract

For the chocolate mousse:
3 cups soy milk
5 ounces dairy-free grain-sweetened
  chocolate chips
3 tablespoons arrowroot
1 teaspoon almond extract
1 tablespoon vanilla extract
3 tablespoons agar flakes
2 tablespoons maple sugar
2 tablespoons maple syrup

For the raspberry syrup:
4 tablespoons organic sugar-free
  raspberry jam
⅓ cup hot water

To make the Lady Fingers and bottom cake:
1. Preheat the oven to 325°F.
2. In a large bowl, combine the dry ingredients.
3. In a medium bowl, emulsify wet ingredients.
4. Using a whisk, blend the wet ingredients into the dry mix. After blending well, use a spatula to give the mixture some air.
5. To make the bottom cake, pour half of the batter into an 6-inch springform pan, using enough batter to fill the bottom.
6. To make the Lady Fingers, place the remaining batter in a pastry bag with a flat tip.
7. Cover a baking pan with waxed paper. Gently squeezing the pastry bag, pipe the cake batter onto the waxed paper in 1 by 4-inch sticks.
8. Bake the bottom cake and the Lady Fingers for 25 to 30 minutes.

continued on next page...

COOKING TIP:
This cake can be made in different sizes. To do so, simply use a different size springform pan. If the pan is larger in diameter and shorter vertically, the Lady Fingers may need to be made smaller to match the height of the cake.

31

continued from previous page...

CHOCOLATE RASPBERRY CHARLOTTE

To make the chocolate mousse:
1. In a saucepan, combine the soy milk, agar and arrowroot over medium heat. Simmer until the agar is dissolved.
2. Add the almond and vanilla extracts along with the chocolate chips. Mix well with a wooden spoon until chocolate has melted.
3. Pour mixture into a blender and blend until smooth, about 1 minute.
4. Set aside and allow to cool for a few minutes.

To make the raspberry syrup:
1. In a small bowl, thoroughly combine the raspberry jam and the boiling water. Set aside.

To complete:
1. Using a pastry brush, dab the cake bottom with the raspberry syrup so that it soaks into the cake.
2. Pour half of the chocolate mousse over the cake bottom.
2. Place a few Lady Fingers over the mousse. Cover with the remainder of the mousse and refrigerate for 2 hours.
4. Using a table knife dipped in hot water, release the cake and mousse from the springform pan edge. Open and remove the outer ring of the pan.
5. Line the Lady Fingers upright around the outer sides of the cake.
6. Arrange the fresh raspberries on top of the mousse.
7. Tie a red ribbon (approximately 30 inches long) around the outer rim of the cake for decoration.

Strawberry Sorbet with Crispy Almonds Tuiles

A light and refreshing dessert with thin crispy tuiles.

MAKES 4 SERVINGS

For the Strawberry Sorbet:
16 ounces frozen organic strawberries
¼ cup maple syrup
1 teaspoon lemon juice
1 pinch sea salt

For the Crispy Almonds Tuiles:
⅓ cup maple sugar
⅓ cup maple syrup
3 ounces non-hydrogenated soy
   margarine
⅔ cup unbleached flour
1 pinch sea salt
⅔ cup sliced almonds

To make the Strawberry Sorbet:
1. Leave the frozen strawberries out at room temperature for 20 minutes.
2. In a food processor, purée the strawberries until smooth.
3. Add the sea salt, lemon juice and maple syrup. Process for a few more seconds.
4. Transfer to a freezer container and freeze (up to 2 weeks).

To make the Crispy Almond Tuiles:
1. Preheat the oven to 350°F.
2. In a large bowl, combine the ingredients to make a dough. Divide and roll dough into 12 balls, about 1-ounce each.
3. On a baking sheet, evenly spread out 6 dough balls.
4. Press on each dough ball to flatten into a 4-inch diameter circle.
5. Bake 6 tuiles per baking sheet for about 8 minutes, or until golden brown.
6. Allow tuiles to cool on the pan.
7. Using a stainless steel spatula, remove tuiles from the baking sheet and set aside. Do not stack them.

To serve:
1. Using an ice cream scoop or 2 soup spoons, make a small ball of the sorbet and set it in the middle of a Crispy Almonds Tuile.
2. Add a second tuile over the ball of sorbet. Add one final scoop of sorbet to crown the dessert.

upside-down berry cake

Originally one of my mom's easy dishes for last minute guests. Serve it warm, and it will disappear.

MAKES 4 TO 6 SERVINGS

For the cake:
½ cup whole wheat pastry flour
½ cup unbleached white flour
½ tablespoon aluminum-free baking powder
⅛ teaspoon sea salt
¼ teaspoon turmeric
¼ cup safflower oil
⅓ cup rice syrup or maple syrup
½ cup soy milk
1 lemon rind, grated
⅓ tablespoon vanilla extract

2 cups organic strawberries, sliced
1 cup organic blueberries
1 cup organic raspberries
or 4 cups frozen mixed berries
(blackberry, blueberry, raspberry)

To make the cake:
1. Preheat the oven to 350°F. Rub a thin coat of oil onto a cake pan.
2. In a large bowl, sift the dry ingredients and whisk.
3. In a separate bowl, whisk the wet ingredients until emulsified.
4. Add the wet mixture to the dry mixture and stir just until combined. Do not over-mix.
5. Combine the berries in an 8 by 8-inch pan and pour the batter over the berries.
6. Bake for 20 minutes. The cake is ready when a bamboo skewer inserted in the center comes out clean.
7. Allow the cake to cool in the pan for 15 minutes.
8. Flip the cake upside-down on a plate, or use a large serving spoon to scoop individual portions from the pan.

Variation: Can also be made using 4 to 6 individual ramekins.

watermelon thyme granite

Pure and simple watermelon goodness.

MAKES 4 TO 6 SERVINGS

For the granite:
24 ounces watermelon, seeded
½ cup rice syrup
1 tablespoon lemon juice
1 tablespoon fresh chopped thyme
4 to 6 sprigs of fresh thyme for garnish

To make the granite:
1. In a blender, purée the watermelon until smooth.
2. Add the lemon juice and rice syrup. Blend briefly.
3. Pour mixture into a large freezer container.
4. Add the chopped thyme, stir to combine and freeze.
5. Using a fork, stir mixture every 30 minutes until set (about 2 to 3 times).
6. When frozen, rake the granite until it becomes loose, like rock salt.
7. Keep frozen until ready to use.
8. Scoop granite into individual bowls and garnish with sprigs of fresh thyme.

ENJOY THIS AUTUMN TEA

Genmaicha (Roasted Brown Rice Tea):
Brown rice is harvested in the fall and makes a
nutty-flavored mellow tea. Try making Genmaicha
at home. Rinse the brown rice, then roast it in a
dry skillet until the rice turns a crispy golden color.
Mix ⅓ roasted brown rice and ⅔ Kukicha (Twig
Tea). Genmaicha can be purchased in natural
foods markets or Japanese markets.

Makes 1 cup
1 tablespoons Genmaicha
1 cup purified water

Bring purified water to a boil. Pour the purified
water over the Genmaicha in a teapot. Let steep
for 5 minutes. Strain and drink hot.

autumn

Apple Symphony

Apple Tart Tatin

Baked Pear with Walnut Stuffing and Crème Anglaise

Pecan Pie

Persimmon Rice Pudding

Simmered Red Apple with Currants and Cinnamon

apple symphony

Four different apple creations in one.

MAKES 4 TO 6 SERVINGS

For the apple terrine:
8 organic Fuji apples
¾ cup rice syrup
¾ cup barley malt
1 pinch sea salt
2 tablespoons kuzu

For the apple chips:
2 organic Fuji apples, sliced thinly
Safflower oil

For the apple sorbet:
16 ounces organic apple sauce
2 tablespoons vanilla extract
¼ cup maple syrup

For the apple coulis:
2 organic green apples
Juice from 1 lemon
½ cup organic apple juice

To make the apple terrine:

1. Peel and core the apples, then cut into 10 wedges.
2. Place the apples in a large pan. Add the barley malt and rice syrup.
3. Bring to a boil. Simmer until the apples are soft but not breaking apart.
4. Using a slotted spoon, remove the apple slices, allowing syrup to remain in the pan.
5. Line a 3 by 5-inch loaf pan with an 18-inch long piece of plastic wrap. Allow the excess plastic wrap to hang over the sides of the pan.
6. Place the apples into the pan. Fold the plastic wrap over, covering the apples.
7. Place a light weight on top of the folded plastic wrap to compact the mixture. Refrigerate for 6 hours.
8. Bring the remaining syrup in the pan to a boil.
9. In a small bowl, dilute the kuzu in 2 tablespoons of water and add to the syrup.
10. Continue cooking until mixture thickens. Remove from heat and set aside.

continued on next page...

COOKING TIP:
If time is an issue, use fresh apples slices instead of making the apple chips. Feel free to use a different sorbet as desired.

continued from previous page...

APPLE SYMPHONY

To make the apple chips:
1. Preheat oven to 100°F. Line a baking sheet with waxed paper.
2. Brush the apple slices with oil on both sides. Place the apple slices on the baking sheet.
3. Cover with another sheet of waxed paper and bake for about 1½ to 2 hours, or until crisp. Set aside.

To make the sorbet:
1. In a mixing bowl, combine the apple sauce with the vanilla and maple syrup.
2. Transfer mixture to an ice cream maker. Follow the manufacture's instructions for making sorbet. (Chilling times may vary, usually 20 to 30 minutes.)

To make the apple coulis :
1. Peel and core the apples. Coursely chop the apples into small pieces. Place in a blender.
2. Add the lemon and apple juice and blend well. Strain contents. Refrigerate.

To serve:
1. Remove the terrine from the loaf pan. Slice into 4 to 6 pieces.
2. Drizzle just enough apple coulis to cover the bottom of an oversized individual serving plate.
3. Place one terrine slice in the center of the plate. Cover with a larger apple chip.
4. Top with one scoop of the sorbet. Cover with another apple chip, making a "sandwich."
5. Add a smaller ½-ounce scoop of sorbet and finish with one last apple chip set vertically to crown the dessert.

apple tart tatin

This was one of my first desserts for Sanae, and simply better than the traditional butter and sugar drenched French tatin.

MAKES 1 PIE

For the quick puff pastry:
1 cup unbleached flour
½ cup pastry flour
5 ounces soy margarine, chilled
2 teaspoons white wine vinegar, chilled
3 ⅓ to 4 ⅔ tablespoons water, chilled

For the apple filling:
12 organic Fuji apples
1 cup rice syrup
1 cup barley malt
1 pinch sea salt
2 tablespoons kuzu

To make the puff pastry dough:
1. Combine the soy margarine and flours in a food processor. Process until mixture resembles a coarse meal, about 10 seconds.
2. Add the vinegar and 3 ⅓ tablespoons chilled water. Pulse for 5 to 6 seconds. Scrape down mixture and pulse for another 3 to 4 seconds. (Dough should just hold together. If mixture is still crumbly, add more chilled water, and pulse an additional 2 to 3 seconds.)
3. Using a rolling pin on a lightly floured surface, roll the dough lengthwise into a rectangle away from you.
4. Fold the ends closest and furthest from you towards the center. Then fold in half, like closing a book, to create 4 layers. Turn 90° and repeat steps (3) and (4).
5. Refrigerate 10 minutes and repeat steps (3) and (4) two more times.
6. Keep refrigerated until use.

continued on next page...

COOKING TIP:
Make sure to cook the apples in a large sauce pan or brazier, because the rice syrup tends to rise quickly and will spill out of a pan that is too small.

continued from previous page...

APPLE TART TATIN

To make the apple filling:
1. Peel, core and cut the apples in half.
2. In a large saucepan, combine the apples, rice syrup, barley malt and sea salt.
3. Bring to a boil and simmer until the apples are soft but not breaking apart.
4. Using a slotted spoon, transfer the apple slices to a 9-inch springform cake pan, allowing syrup to remain in the saucepan.
5. Arrange the apples neatly in a circle on the bottom of the cake pan.
6. Bring the remaining syrup in the pan to a boil.
7. In a small bowl, dilute the kuzu in 2 tablespoons of water and add to the syrup.
8. Continue cooking until mixture thickens.
9. Pour half of the syrup over the apples and set the remaining syrup aside.

To make the Apple Tart Tatin:
1. Preheat the oven to 350°F.
2. Remove the pastry dough from the refrigerator and roll the dough into a shape large enough to cover the pan, ¼-inch thick.
3. Cover the apples with puff pastry dough. Trim off any excess around the rim.
4. Bake for 20 minutes. Remove from the oven and allow pan to cool for 10 minutes.
5. On top of a serving plate, set the pan upside-down. Allow to cool completely before removing the cake pan.
6. Serve with remaining syrup.

baked pear with Walnut Stuffing and Crème Anglaise

Move over apples, pears rule!

MAKES 6 SERVINGS

For the Crème Anglaise:
2 cups soy milk
½ cup rice syrup
¼ vanilla bean, split in half lengthwise
1 tablespoon kuzu
1 pinch sea salt

For the Baked Pear and Walnut Stuffing:
6 organic Bartlett pears
½ cup organic monukka raisins
1 cup walnuts, chopped
¼ cup rice syrup
1 teaspoon cinnamon
½ cup organic apple juice

¼ cup organic apple juice (for baking)

To make the Crème Anglaise:
1. Combine vanilla bean and soy milk in a sauté pan and simmer for 5 minutes.
2. With a slotted spoon, remove the vanilla bean. Scrape the seeds from the bean and pour the seeds back into the soy milk, along with the rice syrup and sea salt.
3. Dissolve the kuzu with 1 tablespoon of water and whisk into the soy milk mixture. Cook over a low flame for 1 minute (do not boil).
4. Transfer the mixture to a container and refrigerate.

To make the Baked Pear and Walnut Stuffing:
1. Soak the raisins in ½ cup of the apple juice for 1 hour.
2. Preheat the oven to 350°F.
3. Slice the bottom of each pear. Using a melon spoon, scoop out the core section of the pear, about half way up the insides of the pear (as shown in photo at left).
4. In a bowl, combine the walnuts, raisins, rice syrup and cinnamon.
5. Stuff all the pears equally. Pack tightly.
6. Place pears cut-side down in a baking pan with ¼ cup of the apple juice. Bake for 30 minutes.
7. Allow to cool and serve with Crème Anglaise.

pecan pie

Sanae goes nuts for this pie.

MAKES 1 PIE

For the pie crust:
1 cup spelt flour
¾ cup unbleached flour
¼ teaspoon sea salt
⅓ cup maple sugar
⅓ cup safflower oil
¼ cup purified water

For the pecan filling:
1 ¼ cups pecans, crushed
2 cups almond-flavored or plain
　　Amazake
½ cup maple sugar
¼ teaspoon sea salt
3 tablespoons safflower oil
1 teaspoon vanilla extract
4 tablespoons agar flakes
3 tablespoons arrowroot

For the pie topping:
1 cup pecans, halved

For the apricot glaze:
3 tablespoons organic sugar-free
　　apricot jam
3 tablespoons water

To make the pie crust:
1. Preheat the oven to 350°F.
2. Combine the dry ingredients in a large bowl.
3. Add the oil and water, and knead quickly to form a dough. Allow dough to sit for 15 minutes.
4. Using a rolling pin, roll the dough into a circle slightly larger than a 9-inch pie pan. (Dough thickness should not exceed ¼-inch).
5. Gently line the pie pan with the dough, trimming off any excess.
6. Bake for 20 to 25 minutes. Remove from the oven and allow to cool.

To make the pecan filling and pie:
1. Roast the pecans until fragrant, about 5 minutes.
2. In a large saucepan, combine all the filling ingredients (except for the halved pecans) and whisk together.
3. Bring to a boil and simmer for 5 minutes until the agar has dissolved.
4. Pour the filling into the pie shell. Arrange the halved pecans on top of the filling. Bake for another 10 minutes.

To make the apricot glaze:
1. In a small saucepan, melt the jam and water together to make a thinner consistency.
2. Glaze the pie then allow to cool.

persimmon rice pudding

We have a persimmon tree in our garden and love the fruit. This recipe uses dried persimmon, which lends a perfect natural sweetness to the pudding.

MAKES 4 SERVINGS

For the pudding:
2 cups soy milk
1 cup cooked brown rice
½ cup dried persimmon
¼ teaspoon cinnamon
1 pinch of ground cardamom
½ tablespoon vanilla extract

To make the pudding:
1. Warm the soy milk in a saucepan over low heat. Stir in the remaining ingredients, cover and cook very gently for 15 to 20 minutes, stirring occasionally. Do not allow the soy milk to boil.
2. When the fruits are plump and soft and most of the milk is absorbed, remove from heat.
3. Serve warm, room temperature or chilled.

simmered red apple with Currants and Cinnamon

This simple dessert was one of my earliest efforts during Sanae's recovery.

MAKES 4 SERVINGS

For the simmered apples:
4 organic apples (Fuji or Ambrosia)
1 ½ cups water
½ cup currants
1 teaspoon cinnamon
1 teaspoon vanilla extract

To make the simmered apples:
1. Peel, core and slice the apples in half.
2. In a sauté pan, place the apple slices cut-side down.
3. Cover with water and bring to a boil.
4. Turn heat down. Simmer for 20 minutes.
5. Add the currants, sprinkle the cinnamon over each apple slice then add the vanilla extract.
6. Cover and simmer 15 minutes more or until the apples are soft when pricked in the center with a bamboo skewer.
7. To serve, arrange 2 apple halves per plate, drizzle with leftover cooking juices and garnish with currants.

ENJOY THIS WINTER BEVERAGE

Grain Coffee:
There are many different nutritious grain "coffees" available in natural foods stores. Made from an assortment of grains, these go well with your pastry and desserts, and they are an excellent source of energy during winter. It's as easy to prepare as instant coffee.

Makes 1 cup
2 teaspoons Grain Coffee (read each product quantity)
1 cup purified water

Put 2 teaspoons Grain Coffee in a cup. Pour one cup boiling purified water into the cup and mix. Serve hot.

winter & holidays

French Canadian Maple Pie

Cashew Crème Brulee

Chocolate Truffles

Classic Baked Tofu Cheesecake

Satsuma Tangerine Poppy Seed Chiffon Cake with Blueberry Stew

french canadian maple pie

This is in memory of my late grandmother, who made it for me almost every week. I present it to you without cream and brown sugar.

MAKES 1 PIE

For the pate sucree:
1 ½ cups pastry flour
¼ cup maple sugar
1 pinch sea salt
¼ cup safflower oil
⅓ cup cold water

For the maple filling:
2 cups Amazake
1 cup maple syrup
¼ teaspoon sea salt
2 tablespoons safflower oil
1 teaspoon vanilla extract
4 tablespoons agar flakes
3 tablespoons arrowroot

To make the pate sucree:
1. Preheat the oven to 350°F.
2. Combine the dry ingredients in a large bowl.
3. Add the oil and water, and knead quickly to form a dough. Allow dough to sit for 15 minutes.
4. Using a rolling pin, roll the dough into a circle slightly larger than an 8-inch pie pan. (Dough thickness should not exceed ¼-inch).
5. Gently line the pie pan with the dough, trimming off any excess. Cut leaf shapes out of the excess dough to use as garnish and place on a baking sheet.
6. Bake pie shell and leaf shapes at the same time for 20 to 25 minutes. Remove from the oven. Allow to cool.

To make the maple filling and pie:
1. In a large saucepan, whisk together the filling ingredients.
2. Bring to a boil. Simmer 5 minutes (until the agar is dissolved).
3. Pour the filling into the pie shell, decorate with baked leaf-shapes. Allow to cool.

cashew crème brulee

There is a crème brulee recipe in every dessert cook book, so here is a great dairy and egg free one!

MAKES 4 SERVINGS

For the crème brulee:

1 ½ cups water
½ cup raw cashews
1 tablespoon agar flakes
⅛ teaspoon sea salt
¼ teaspoon vanilla extract
¼ cup maple sugar
6 ounces soft silken tofu
   (Mori-Nu brand)

For caramelized topping:

6 teaspoons maple sugar

To make the crème brulee:

1. In a blender or food processor, combine cashews, agar and salt. Process to fine crumbs.
2. Bring the water to a boil.
3. Pour ½ cup of the boiling water into the blender mixture and process for about 1 minute. Gradually add remaining boiling water, then process on high for 2 more minutes.
4. Add vanilla, maple sugar and tofu and process for 1 more minute.
5. Transfer mixture to a saucepan. Cook over low heat, stirring constantly, for 10 to 15 minutes. Do not allow mixture to boil.
6. Distribute mixture evenly among four 4-inch ramekins. Allow to cool at room temperature, then refrigerate until chilled.
7. To serve, sprinkle the custard with maple sugar and caramelize with a blow torch.

chocolate truffles

Wow, what a treat! No explanation needed.

MAKES 24 TRUFFLES

For the truffles:
1 cup soy milk
18 ounces dairy-free, grain-sweetened
   chocolate chips
2 tablespoons agar flakes
1 tablespoon cocoa powder

For the coating:
Cocoa powder
Roasted hazelnuts, finely chopped
Roasted coconut flakes

To make the truffles:
1. In a saucepan over medium heat, bring the soy milk and agar to a simmer.
2. Add the chocolate chips and stir well until melted.
3. Remove from heat, transfer mixture to a baking pan. Allow to cool, then refrigerate for 1 hour.
4. Using a spoon, scoop up about 1-ounce of the chocolate mixture. Roll between your hands to form a small ball. Continue until mixture is used up.
5. Roll each ball in the cocoa powder, chopped hazelnuts or coconut flakes.
6. Store in the refrigerator until ready to serve.

classic baked tofu cheesecake

I remember the first time I made this Tofu Cheesecake. Sanae loved it and said "my grandmother in heaven will be knocked out of her socks."

MAKES 1 CHEESECAKE

For the granola crust:
½ cup organic corn oil
¼ cup barley malt
¼ cup maple syrup
¼ cup organic apple juice
½ cup walnuts, chopped
4 cups rolled oats
½ tablespoon cinnamon, ground
½ cup almond slices

For the cheesecake filling:
2 lbs. soft silken tofu (Nasoya brand)
1 ½ cups maple syrup
1 tablespoon vanilla extract
2 tablespoons sesame butter
1 pinch sea salt
¼ cup lemon juice
1 teaspoon lemon rind, grated
3 tablespoons arrowroot
2 tablespoons agar flakes
¼ cup organic apple juice

To make the granola crust:
1. Preheat the oven to 325°F.
2. In a mixing bowl, combine the ingredients and transfer to a baking pan.
3. Bake for 15 minutes, mixing occasionally.
4. Remove from oven, break the granola up into pieces and allow to cool.
5. Combine 2 cups of the granola with 2 tablespoons each of the corn oil, apple juice, and maple syrup.
6. Press the granola mixture into the base of an 9-inch springform pan. Set aside.

To make the cheesecake filling:
1. Increase oven temperature to 350°F.
2. Crumble tofu into a blender and add all remaining ingredients. Blend well, stopping a few times to mix the contents with a spatula, to achieve an even, creamy consistency.
3. Pour filling into the crust and bake for 45 to 50 minutes.
4. Allow to cool and serve with your favorite topping.

Satsuma tangerine chiffon cake

with Blueberry Stew

Tangy and sweet, also good for breakfast muffins.

MAKES 12 INDIVIDUAL SERVINGS

For the cake:
1 ½ cups whole wheat pastry flour
1 ½ cups unbleached white flour
1 ½ tablespoons aluminum-free baking
   powder
½ teaspoon sea salt
2 tablespoons poppy seeds
¼ teaspoon turmeric
½ cup safflower oil
1 cup rice syrup or maple syrup
1 cup soy milk
1 grated Satsuma tangerine rind
½ cup Satsuma tangerine juice
½ cup Satsuma tangerine sections
1 teaspoon vanilla extract

For the Blueberry Stew:
2 cups fresh organic blueberries
2 cups organic apple juice
½ tablespoon kuzu

For the Soy Vanilla Cream:
2 cups soy milk
¼ cup rice syrup
½ vanilla bean
2 tablespoons kuzu
1 pinch sea salt

To make the cake:
1. Preheat the oven to 350°F. Rub a thin coat of oil onto a muffin pan.
2. In a large bowl, sift the dry ingredients and whisk.
3. In a separate bowl, whisk the wet ingredients and the grated rind until emulsified.
4. Add the wet mixture to the dry flour mixture and whisk gently. Add the orange sections. Stir to combine.
5. Pour batter into a muffin pan and bake for 25 minutes. The cakes are ready when a bamboo skewer inserted in the center comes out clean.
6. Allow cakes to cool for 10 minutes, then remove from the pan. Set them on a cooling rack. Allow to cool completely.

To make the Blueberry Stew:
1. Dilute the kuzu in the apple juice. Bring to a simmer. It will get thick after a few minutes.
2. Add the blueberries and mix with a wooden spoon. Set aside.

To make the Soy Vanilla Cream:
1. Split the vanilla bean lengthwise with a knife, add to the soy milk and bring to simmer.
2. With a slotted spoon, remove the vanilla bean. Scrape the seeds from the beans and pour the seeds back into the soy milk. Add the rice syrup and sea salt.
3. In a small bowl, dissolve the kuzu root in 2 tablespoons of water. Whisk kuzu into the soy milk mixture for a few minutes. Transfer to a container and refrigerate.

To serve:
In the center of an individual plate, pour 2 ounces of Soy Vanilla Cream. Place an individual Satsuma Chiffon Tangerine Cake in the center of the cream and top with Blueberry Stew.

69

ENJOY THIS TEA ANYTIME

Kukicha (Twig Tea):
This delicious, nutritious tea has a delightfully
refreshing aroma. It is the tea that will satisfy your
senses and body during all seasons, every day.
It is perfect with any of my pastries and desserts.

Makes 1 cup
2 teaspoons Kukicha (Twig Tea)
1 cup purified water

Bring purified water to a boil. Pour the purified
water over the Kukicha (Twig Tea) in a teapot and
let steep for 5 minutes. Strain and drink hot.

all seasons

Black Sesame Biscotti or Almond Anise Biscotti

Azuki Rolls

Coconut Macaroons

Kabocha Poundcake

Lavender Sablé Cookies or Sesame Sablé Cookies

Graham Apple Sage Squares or Rosemary Squares

Tiramisu

black sesame biscotti

or Almond Anise Biscotti

Traditional and easy to make.

MAKES 24 BISCOTTI

For the biscotti:
1 ½ cups pastry flour
1 ½ cups unbleached flour
½ tablespoon aluminum-free baking powder
⅛ tablespoon sea salt
¼ cup maple sugar
⅔ cup soy milk
1 ½ teaspoons kuzu
¼ cup rice syrup or maple syrup
¼ cup safflower oil
1 teaspoon vanilla extract
1 teaspoon lemon juice

For Black Sesame Biscotti:
½ cup black sesame seeds

For Almond Anise Biscotti:
2 cups whole roasted almonds
1 ½ tablespoons anise seed

To make the biscotti:
1. Preheat the oven to 325°F.
2. In a large bowl, combine the dry ingredients. Add your choice of black sesame seeds or almonds / anise seeds to the dry ingredients.
3. In a separate bowl, whisk the wet ingredients until emulsified.
4. Add the wet mixture to the dry flour mixture and combine well by hand.
5. Separate the dough into 2 halves. Using your hands, form 2 logs, each about 4 by 10 inches.
6. Press each log down firmly so that the bottom side of the biscotti will be flat. Pull in both sides of the dough log with your hands so that the edges do not become too thin.
7. Bake for 20 minutes. Cut each log into 12 slices and bake for another 10 minutes on each side.

azuki rolls

Japan's favorite beans with an American twist.

MAKES 8 ROLLS

For the azuki filling:
1 cup azuki beans, dried
3 cups purified water
½ cup rice syrup
pinch of sea salt
¼ cup maple sugar

For the dough:
2 ½ cups unbleached flour
¼ teaspoon sea salt
1 ¼ tablespoons aluminum-free baking
　powder
½ teaspoon baking soda
¾ cup safflower oil
1 ¼ cups soy milk
1 tablespoon apple cider vinegar

For the apricot glaze:
½ cup sugar-free apricot jam
½ cup organic apple juice

To make the azuki filling:
1. In a saucepan, combine azuki beans, water, rice syrup and sea salt.
2. Bring to a boil, cover and simmer for 75 minutes.
3. Transfer mixture to a food processor and partially purée for a few seconds.

To make the dough:
1. In a small mixing bowl, combine all the dry ingredients with a whisk.
2. In a separate bowl, whisk the wet ingredients until emulsified.
3. Add the wet mixture to the dry flour mixture to combine. Mixture will form a lightly sticky, very delicate dough. (Handle with care.)

To make the Azuki Rolls:
1. Preheat oven to 375°F.
2. Transfer the dough to a lightly floured surface and knead until smooth, adding more flour if needed.
3. Roll the dough on a lightly floured surface to form an 8 by 16-inch rectangle. Add flour for rolling if needed; the dough should still be very sticky.
4. Cover the dough with about 1 cup of the pureed azuki, leaving a 2-inch border along the short side. Sprinkle azuki with maple sugar.
5. Roll up the dough lengthwise, towards the 2-inch border. Seal the border and pinch the dough closed.
6. Cut the dough crosswise into 1-inch thick slices.
7. Place each slice on a baking sheet lined in waxed paper. Bake for 23 to 25 minutes or until lightly browned.

To make the apricot glaze:
1. Dilute the jam with the apple juice to make a thin consistency.
2. Using a pastry brush, glaze each baked Azuki Roll. Store at room temperature.

kabocha pound cake

This is a favorite of mine when I travel to Japan.
I hope you will enjoy it, too.

MAKES 1 LOAF

For the Kabocha Pound Cake:
⅓ cup safflower oil
½ cup organic apple sauce
2 ounces firm tofu
¼ cup organic apple juice
½ cup soy milk
¾ cup maple syrup
¾ cup whole wheat pastry flour
¾ cup unbleached flour
½ tablespoon aluminum-free baking
   powder
1 pinch baking soda
1 pinch sea salt
1 cup kabocha squash, diced and
   steamed

To make the Kabocha Pound Cake:
1. Preheat the oven to 325°F.
2. In a blender, combine the wet ingredients and blend until smooth.
3. In a small mixing bowl, combine the dry ingredients with a whisk.
4. Whisk the wet mixture into the dry mixture until well combined. Add ¾ cup of the kabocha and stir.
5. Pour batter into a loaf pan.
6. Sprinkle remaining kabocha cubes on top of the batter.
7. Bake for 25 to 35 minutes. The cake is ready when a bamboo skewer inserted in the center comes out clean.

Coconut Macaroons

This tasty little dessert is a perfect party food. Simple to make and oh, so good!

MAKES 36 COOKIES

For the macaroons:
12 ounces shredded dry coconut
2 tablespoons organic soy milk
⅔ cup rice syrup (10 tablespoons)

To make the macaroons:
1. Preheat the oven at 350°F .
2. In a bowl, combine the soy milk and the coconut.
3. Add the rice syrup and mix with a wooden spoon.
4. Form triangles of ⅓ ounce each, or use a small ice cream scoop.
5. Bake on a waxed-paper lined baking sheet for 12 to 15 minutes.
6. Allow the macaroons to cool before removing from baking sheet.

lavender sablé cookies

or Sesame Sablé Cookies

I made these for our wedding guests as favors.
They are as sweet as everlasting love.

MAKES ABOUT 24 COOKIES

For the cookies:
¼ cup safflower oil
¼ cup maple syrup
1 tablespoon rice syrup
1 tablespoon tahini
¾ cup whole wheat pastry flour
½ cup unbleached flour
1 teaspoon aluminum-free baking
  powder
⅛ teaspoon sea salt

For the Sesame Sablé Cookies:
½ cup sesame seeds, lightly roasted

For the Lavender Sablé Cookies:
1 tablespoon organic lavender flowers*

*Do not use lavender from a florist. Choose
home-grown or organically grown flowers.

To make the cookies:
1. Preheat the oven to 350°F.
2. In a bowl, whisk the wet ingredients.
3. Sift all dry ingredients in a bowl.
4. Add the sesame seeds or lavender flowers and whisk until well combined.
5. Using a spatula, add the wet ingredients to the dry ingredients. Stir until texture resembles a smooth paste.
6. Divide the dough into four pieces. Roll each piece into a log, 2 inches in diameter, by hand on a flat smooth surface. Enclose each log in plastic wrap and refrigerate for 2 hours.
7. Cover a baking sheet with waxed paper. Slice the dough logs into ¾-inch pieces and place them on the baking sheet.
8. Bake for 8 minutes. Turn the cookies over carefully. Continue baking for another 8 minutes or until light golden in color.
9. Allow cookies to cool completely, then store them in a sealed container where they will keep for up to 3 weeks.

81

graham apple sage squares
or Rosemary Squares

Great for afternoon tea and enhanced with flavors from our garden.

MAKES 24 COOKIES

For the graham squares:
1 cup whole wheat pastry flour
1 cup rolled oats
1 cup slivered almonds
¼ teaspoon aluminum-free baking powder
½ teaspoon sea salt
3 tablespoons apple sage or rosemary, chopped
½ cup safflower oil
½ cup maple syrup
1 teaspoon vanilla extract

To make the graham squares:
1. Preheat the oven to 375°F.
2. In a large bowl, sift the dry ingredients and whisk.
3. In a separate bowl, whisk the wet ingredients until emulsified.
4. Add the wet mixture to the dry mixture and stir until combined into a dough.
5. Divide the dough into two halves. One at a time, roll each half between 2 sheets of waxed paper to form a ¼-inch thick rectangle (approximately the size of a halfsheet pan).
6. Remove the top sheet of waxed paper and pre-cut the dough into 2 by 2-inch squares. Remove any excess trimmings.
7. Leaving the cookies and bottom sheet of waxed paper in place on the pan, bake for 12 minutes, or until a light golden color.
8. Allow to cool and separate into pieces along the pre-cut lines. Cookies will keep for up to 1 week.

tiramisu

The perfect Italian dessert with a soybean base.

MAKES 4 TO 6 SERVINGS

For the cake:
¾ cup pastry flour
1 ¼ cups unbleached flour
½ teaspoon sea salt
¾ teaspoon baking soda
¼ cup safflower oil
⅜ cup soy milk
¾ cup maple syrup
½ teaspoon apple cider vinegar
½ tablespoon vanilla extract

For the tofu cream:
30 ounces firm tofu (Mori-Nu brand)
1 cup maple sugar
1 pinch sea salt
1 tablespoon vanilla extract
1 tablespoon tahini
2 tablespoons arrowroot
1 tablespoon lemon juice

For the espresso syrup:
1 cup hot water
8 teaspoons grain coffee (Yannoh brand)
2 tablespoons maple syrup

¼ cup cocoa powder, for garnish

To make the cake:
1. Preheat the oven to 325°F.
2. In a large bowl, whisk together the dry ingredients.
3. In a separate bowl, whisk the wet ingredients until emulsified.
4. Using a spatula, add the wet mixture to the dry mixture and stir until combined.
5. Cover a halfsheet pan with waxed paper and spread with the cake batter, ½-inch thick.
6. Bake for 25 to 30 minutes. The cake is ready when a bamboo skewer inserted in the center comes out clean.

To make the tofu cream:
1. Blanche the tofu in a pan of hot water for 1 minute.
2. Dry tofu by pressing between towels and place in a food processor.
3. Add the remaining ingredients and process until smooth and creamy. Set aside.

To make the espresso syrup:
1. In a small bowl, pour in the hot water. Add grain coffee and maple syrup and stir to combine. Set aside.

To assemble the Tiramisu:
1. Slice the cake in 2 halves.
2. In a 9 by 12-inch pan, place one layer of cake as the bottom layer.
3. Using a pastry brush, soak the bottom cake with half of the the espresso syrup.
4. Evenly spread half of the tofu cream mixture over the soaked cake.
5. Add the second layer of cake, and brush again with the remaining espresso syrup.
6. Spread the remaining tofu cream ontop.
7. Dust with cocoa powder, and refrigerate for 2 hours.

BASIC ESSENTIALS

Springform cake pan, 6-inch and 9-inch
Loaf pan, 4 by 8-inch
Half sheet pan / baking pan, 12 by 17-inch
Muffin pan
Tart rings / pans, 9-inch
Ramekins, shallow 4-inch

Silpat nonstick baking mat
Wax paper
Pastry brush
Melon scoop
Whisk
Peeler
Corer
Grater
Zester
Bamboo skewers

Food processor
Blender
Ice cream machine
Butane torch

METRIC CONVERSION

Temperature
Fahrenheit to Celsius

F	C
200 – 205	95
229 – 225	105
245 – 250	120
275	135
300 – 305	150
325 – 330	165
345 – 350	175
370 – 375	190
400 – 405	205
425 – 430	220
445 – 450	230
470 – 475	245
500	260

Liquid And Dry Measures

US	Metric
¼ teaspoon	1.25 milliliters
½ teaspoon	2.5 milliliters
1 teaspoon	5 milliliters
1 tablespoon	15 milliliters
¼ cup	60 milliliters
⅓ cup	80 milliliters
1 cup	240 milliliters
1 pint (2 cups)	480 milliliters
1 quart (4 cups)	960 milliliters
1 gallon (4 quarts)	3.84 liters
1 ounce (oz.)	28 grams
1 pound (16 oz.)	454 grams
2.2 pounds	1 kilogram

Length Measures

US	Metric
⅛ inch	3 millimeters
¼ inch	6 millimeters
½ inch	12 millimeters
1 inch	2.5 centimeters

INDEX

GLOSSARY

Agar agar
A sea vegetable that comes in bar or flake form. Used for making gelatins and aspics.

Almonds
Fruit kernels of the almond tree. They keep best when purchased in their brown skins, which protect freshness and flavor.

Amazake
A sweetener or refreshing drink made from sweet brown rice and koji starter that is allowed to ferment into a thick liquid.

Arrowroot
A starch obtained from the roots of various tropical plants. Excellent natural thickening agent for soups, sauces and other cooked foods in lieu of flour or cornstarch. Tasteless. Becomes clear when cooked.

Azuki (Adzuki or Aduki) beans
A small, dark red bean originally from Japan but also now grown in the United States. Similar to a kidney bean, only more flavorful.

Baking powder (aluminum-free)
A leavening agent made up of baking soda, cream of tartar, and either cornstarch or arrowroot. It releases carbon dioxide upon contact with liquid, creating air pockets which create the light texture in baked goods.

Barley flour
Flour made from barley, which can give breads or pancakes a cake-like texture and a pleasant, nutty sweetness. Also sometimes used as a thickener.

Barley malt
A sweetener made from barley. Great in desserts, bean dishes and tea.

Brown rice
Whole, unpolished rice, containing an ideal balance of minerals protein, and carbohydrates.

Brown rice flour
A nuttier and richer tasting flour, more nutritious than the white rice variety. Brown rice flour can be used for breads, cakes, muffins, and noodles. It contains no gluten.

Cashew
A tropical nut high in fat, with a rich, luscious flavor for creams and nut milks.

Crème Anglaise
A light pastry cream usually served to complement a dessert.

Charlotte
A creamy mousse cake.

Grain Coffee
A coffee substitute made of roasted grains, beans and roots. It contains no caffeine. It is considered an occasional beverage.

Granite
A crushed ice dessert saturated with flavoring. Softer than a traditional American snow-cone.

Grapeseed oil
Oil high in linoleic acid and low in saturated fats. Good for cooking, with a light, nutty taste.

Hazelnuts
Also known as filberts, these are nuts shaped like large chickpeas. They have a very bitter outer skin that must be removed before eating.

Kanten
A gelled dessert made from agar agar.

Kuzu
A white starch made from the root of a wild plant. Also known as kudzu.

Maple syrup
The boiled-down sap of the sugar maple which can be used as a natural flavoring and sweetener. Do not confuse this with "maple-flavored" syrup, which is usually mostly sugar or corn syrup.

Maple sugar
A concentrated, crystallized form of maple syrup.

Meiwa kumquat
One of the sweetest kumquats, and known as the best for eating by itself. Kumquats are similar to very tiny, orange, soft-skinned grapefruits. They ripen in early spring.

Meyer lemon
A variant of a common lemon, originally from China, that is a cross with a tangerine. They are rounder than common lemons and have thin, soft, smooth rinds, which are a rich yellow-orange when fully ripe. The pulp is deep yellow and low in acid.

Millet flour
A gluten-free flour alternative, ground from whole millet, that adds a nut-like, slightly sweet flavor to wheat breads.

Mochi
A rice cake or dumpling made from cooked, pounded sweet rice.

Oat flour
Flour made from grinding oat groats to a fine consistency. This may be done on your own by grinding rolled oats in a blender. It is very low in gluten, so add a gluten-containing flour with it to help your bread rise.

Pain Perdu
French toast.

Persimmon
Japanese Fuyu persimmons are squat, orange-like fruits with red-orange skin and papery leaves. The Fuyu variety is sweet and square-shaped, as opposed to the very acidic and triangular Hachiya variety. Both of these are larger than the less common American varieties.

Pine nuts
An edible seed found inside pine cones. They have a soft texture and sweet flavor.

Rice syrup
A sweetener made by fermenting brown rice.

Sablé (sah-BLAY)
A sweet, dry cookie, like shortbread.

Safflower oil
Great for cooking, baking, or as a salad oil.

Sea salt
Salt obtained from the ocean and either sun-baked or kiln-baked. Unlike refined table salt, it is high in trace minerals and contains no chemicals, sugar or other additives.

Soy flour
Ground from raw soybeans, soy flour is rich in calcium, iron and protein, and is gluten-free. Tends to add a slightly sweet, pleasant flavor to breads. Soya flour is the same, but is made from lightly toasted soybeans instead of raw ones.

Soy milk
The rich, creamy milk of whole soybeans. Usually sold as "soy beverage" or "soy drink," it is an excellent dairy substitute and is high in B-vitamins and protein.

Spelt flour
Made from a non-hybridized wheat, it works well as a bread flour and is very high in protein and fiber. It is a good substitute for some people who are allergic to wheat.

Spring Lady peach
Originally from China, peaches are medium-sized, round fruits with fuzzy skins. The Spring Lady is a variety of semi-freestone peach (where the flesh pulls away from the seed) that is in season in the spring through summer.

Sunflower oil
Mild in flavor, good for most uses except for deep frying.

Tahini
A seed butter made from grinding sesame seeds until smooth and creamy.

Tofu
Soybean curd made from soybeans and nigari, low in calories, saturated fats, and cholesterol. Tofu is very versatile. It can be fried, baked, added raw to soups and salads, or ground up and used as a dairy substitute.

Tuiles
A thin, crispy cookie studded with almonds that is easy to form into different shapes while hot from the oven.

Tumeric
A dark yellow spice from India, similar to ginger, that is a major ingredient in Indian curry and Worcestershire sauce.

Unbleached white flour
Popular due to its versatility, white flour can be used for breads, pastries, cookies, and cakes. To enhance its nutritional quality, substitute part of the white flour with whole wheat flour.

Vanilla extract
A smoky, smooth flavoring made by extracting the essence from vanilla beans. You can get vanilla extract preserved with or without alcohol.

Whole wheat pastry flour
Soft whole wheat flour that is milled from soft winter wheat berries, different than those used for bread-making. Whole wheat pastry flour can absorb large amounts of fat, and does not rise like other flour, which make it ideal for pastry and cake making.